# The Incredible ICE CREAM Book

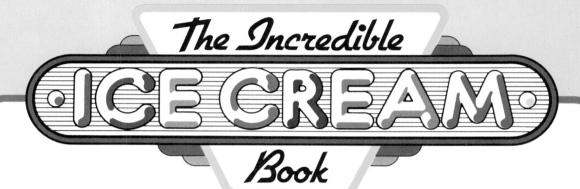

by
## Dennis J. Willard

To My Wife Tina.
Thanks for your love, support,
and taste buds.

Glassware courtesy, Anchor Hocking Glass Co.

Published by Willowisp Press, Inc.
401 E. Wilson Bridge Road, Worthington, Ohio 43085

Printed in the United States of America
10 9 8 7 6 5 4 3 2 1

ISBN 0-87406-392-2

# Table of Contents

# Smooth and Creamy, Cold and Sweet Ice Cream Has It All

Are tasty sundaes, ice cream sandwiches, thick milk shakes, and bubbly sodas tops on your list of scrumptious treats? Ice cream in any form can be a bundle of fun—both to make and to eat. With a little imagination and a zap of creativity, you can make a variety of dreamy ice cream desserts right at home.

Cooking up these delicacies—from basic milk shakes to a pralines and cream pie—really is a snap. This book is filled with a delicious selection of recipes to let you get a good taste of everyone's favorite dessert.

Ice cream and other frozen delights have been around for centuries. It was actually more than 2,000 years ago when Greeks and Romans began pouring fruit juices over ice. Alexander the Great, a famous Greek ruler, once had his men dig 30 trenches and fill them with snow. Each day, his cooks used the snow to make ice desserts for Alexander and his army. The ditches were covered with branches to keep the sun out.

4

Nero, a Roman emperor, loved ices flavored with fruit juices and honey. But Nero had two problems. Rome did not have any snow or ice, and refrigerators had not yet been invented. So, Nero ordered runners to race to the Alps and gather snow. The Alps are snow-covered mountains hundreds of miles north of Rome in Italy. The runners carried snow for miles before handing it to another runner. This chain of runners finally arrived in Rome, and Nero had fruit-flavored ice for dessert.

When Marco Polo returned to Italy after exploring China, he talked about seeing and tasting creamy desserts made with milk. In the 13th century, Italians were already making icy treats. Marco Polo's tales led them to begin using milk to make ice cream.

Swank ice cream parlors sprang up throughout Europe in the early 1800s. In 1860, Carlo Gatti came to England from Italy to peddle ice cream from his bright cart. He used a hand freezer, and eventually added employees to help him.

In the United States, George Washington was an early fan of ice cream. President Washington had two pewter pots that he ate ice cream from in his Mt. Vernon home. And Dolly Madison, wife of President James Madison, was the first person to serve ice cream in the White House. At this time, ice cream was still considered exotic because it was difficult to make.

In the 19th and 20th centuries, ice cream's popularity grew worldwide. Refrigerators were invented, and ice cream became less expensive to make. As more people were able to afford this delicacy, parlors and soda fountains sprang up in towns and cities everywhere.

Traditional ice cream treats, like the ice cream soda and sundae, became so popular that new delicacies were invented for variety. Among these creations were banana splits, ice cream cones, and ice cream sandwiches.

Today, nearly everyone around the world loves ice cream. Because of a greater awareness of the link between our diets and our health, ice cream now is made with tastier and healthier ingredients than ever before. This link also has led to the development of sherbets, sorbets, yogurts, and ices. These offer sweetness with fewer calories. So, in a sense, Nero's days have come full circle. People again are appreciating the fruit-flavored ices he enjoyed nearly 2,000 years ago.

So, let's get going! Delicious treats await you! All you need are a few fun recipes, the right ingredients, and the patience to wait until your dessert is ready before you dig in!

# Ice Cream Tools

Creating special ice cream desserts definitely is a lot of fun. There are so many combinations you can try, and different ways to decorate your creations! But before you begin your own ice cream masterpiece, read through the recipe that you have selected. Then gather together all the ingredients and equipment you will need.

Some of the utensils needed to prepare the recipes in this book include:

Cookie sheet
Cutting board
Double boiler
Dry-ingredient
  measuring cups
Electric blender
Frozen juice sticks
Ice cream machine
Ice cream scoop
Knife
Large spoons
Liquid measuring cup
Measuring spoons
Medium mixing bowl
Medium saucepan

Melon ball scoop
Parfait glasses
Pie pans
Pot holders
Rolling pin
Round ice cream bowl
Small mixing bowl
Small paper cups
Small saucepan
Soda spoons
Soda straws
Sundae boat
Wax paper
Wire whisk

# Helpful Hints
# To Get You Started

Before you create the ice cream treat you've selected, read through these cooking tips to be sure you are fully prepared.

1. Let your mother or father know if you are planning to cook in the kitchen. They even may want to hang around to lick the fudge bowls!
2. Ask your mother or father to show you how to use the stove, blender, or ice cream machine.
3. Make sure you have all the ingredients you need to prepare the recipe before your taste buds get too excited about the treat!
4. Get out all the equipment (bowls, measuring spoons, scoop, etc.) that you will need for the recipe before you actually begin cooking.
5. Use a dry-ingredient measuring cup for sugar, flour, or any other ingredients that are not liquid.
6. A liquid measuring cup should be used for milk, juices, or anything that needs to be poured.
7. When cooking on the stove, be careful not to touch your hands or arms on the burner. If you will be using a gas stove, keep your hair well away from the flame.

8. Always turn the handles of saucepans and double boilers toward the surface of the stove. If the handle should stick out from the front of the stove, you could bump it and knock hot fudge all over the floor—or worse, on you!

9. When you lift the lid off a saucepan, always lift it away from you. This way the steam will not rise directly at you and possibly burn your face or hands. *Remember: steam is even hotter than boiling water, so be careful.*

10. Handle any saucepan or lid that becomes hot with a pot holder to avoid burning your hands.

11. Before you use a blender, make sure the base is twisted securely onto the glass container. Also, handle the blades carefully to avoid cutting yourself.

12. When you are ready to blend something, put the lid securely on top of the blender. Blending without the lid may result in getting a milk shake all over the kitchen and you, instead of in a glass where you can enjoy it!

13. Clean up the kitchen when you finish cooking. Your mother or father will really appreciate this, and they will be more likely to let you use the kitchen to prepare future treats.

14. Use a damp dishcloth to wipe counter tops. Allow the stove to cool completely before wiping the surface with the dishcloth.

# Super Sundaes

Dripping with sweet toppings and garnished with nuts and cherries, the ice cream sundae will celebrate its gala 100th birthday during the 1990s. Where did the name "sundae" come from to describe this colorful, gooey treat? One story says that the sundae was developed almost by accident.

This ice cream story takes place in Two Rivers, Wisconsin, during the 1890s. A young boy walked into an ice cream shop and ordered a dish of ice cream. He asked the man behind the counter to squirt some chocolate syrup on top. After watching the boy devour the ice cream, the vendor decided it was a great idea. He began selling ice cream with syrup for a nickel on Sundays, so he called them "Sundays."

The ice cream "Sunday" became very popular, and the vendor began to sell the dish every day of the week. He changed the spelling to sundae so that his customers would realize they were available every day.

The sundae definitely has come a long way in less than 100 years. Today, there are dozens of toppings and hundreds of variations that you can choose from. As you will see, sundaes are easy to make. Once you have tried out these recipes, try creating some of your own combinations.

# DINOSAUR'S DELIGHT

## To prepare:
Pour 1/4 cup (60 ml) of hot fudge into the parfait glass. Top this with 1 tbsp. (15 g) of Spanish peanuts, followed by a scoop of vanilla ice cream.

Layer again with 1/4 cup (60 ml) of hot fudge, 1 tbsp. (15 g) of peanuts, and the second scoop of ice cream. Finish with 1/4 cup (60 ml) of hot fudge. Swirl with whipped cream, and garnish with a maraschino cherry.

* To make homemade toppings for this recipe, see the toppings chapter in this book.

## Ingredients:
2 scoops vanilla ice cream

3/4 cup (180 ml)
   hot fudge topping*

3 tbsp. (45 g)
   Spanish peanuts

Whipped cream

1 maraschino cherry

*E*ven a dinosaur has to give in to his sweet tooth now and then. You will never forget this Dinosaur's Delight Parfait, even after the last bite is gone.

# APPLE SPICE & EVERYTHING NICE PARFAIT

## To prepare:
Spread a layer of cinnamon topping on the bottom of each parfait glass. Place a scoop of ice cream in each glass, and sprinkle apple over the top.

Pour the rest of the cinnamon topping over the apple, and follow with another scoop of ice cream. Swirl the whipped cream on top, and garnish the whole thing with the crumb cake.

* To make homemade toppings for this recipe, see the toppings chapter in this book.

## Ingredients:
4 scoops Dutch apple
   ice cream

1/2 cup (120 ml)
   cinnamon topping*

1/2 apple, diced

Whipped cream

4 tbsp. (60 g)
   crumb cake

*T*his is a wild and spicy treat for the daring parfait maker. Your taste buds will be tingling from your first bite of this parfait to the last. This recipe makes two delicious parfaits.

## To prepare:

Place the two scoops of ice cream in a banana split boat. Slice the banana lengthwise, and spread the peanut butter along the flat side of the banana slices. Set one half of the banana on each side of the ice cream scoops.

Pour the hot fudge topping over the chocolate-chip ice cream, and the marshmallow topping over the chocolate peanut butter chunk ice cream.

Swirl some whipped cream on top of each scoop. Finish the dessert off by sprinkling some candy-coated peanut butter pieces over everything.

* To make homemade toppings for this recipe, see the toppings chapter in this book.

## Ingredients:

- 1 scoop chocolate peanut butter chunk ice cream
- 1 scoop chocolate-chip ice cream
- 1/4 cup (60 ml) hot fudge topping*
- 1/4 cup (60 ml) marshmallow topping*
- 1 banana, split in half
- Peanut butter
- Whipped cream
- 2 tbsp. (30 g) candy-coated peanut butter pieces

*A*liens like the classic banana split, except for the one thing that's missing... candy-coated peanut butter pieces! Alien life forms will become very friendly once they discover you are making this sundae.

## To prepare:

Place the three scoops of ice cream in a banana split boat. Slice the banana lengthwise, and set one half on each side of the ice cream scoops.

Pour the chocolate topping over the vanilla ice cream, the marshmallow topping over the chocolate ice cream, and the strawberry topping over the strawberry ice cream.

Then swirl the whipped cream on top of each scoop, and sprinkle nuts over the whole thing. For the perfect finish, place a maraschino cherry in the whipped cream on top of each scoop.

## Tasty tips:

Try substituting different toppings for the scoops of ice cream. Great flavors to try include pineapple, butterscotch, and blueberry.*

\* To make homemade toppings for this recipe, see the toppings chapter in this book.

## Ingredients:

1 scoop vanilla ice cream
1 scoop strawberry ice cream
1 scoop chocolate ice cream
1/4 cup (60 ml) chocolate topping*
1/4 cup (60 ml) marshmallow topping*
1/4 cup (60 ml) strawberry topping*
1 banana, split in half
Whipped cream
3 tbsp. (45 g) chopped nuts
3 maraschino cherries

*T*he banana split is the ultimate *fun*-damental dish for enjoying ice cream. Since the beginning of this century, ice cream fans have been using this classic recipe to make the world's most famous sundae.

**Fun Facts**

The world's longest banana split was 4 miles in length. It was constructed by the Zeta Beta Tau fraternity of Bowling Green State University in Bowling Green, Ohio, U.S.A. on August 25, 1985. This fact is according to the 1988 edition of the *Guinness Book of World Records*.

# MAGIC MALTED PARFAIT

## To prepare:

Put a scoop of ice cream into each parfait glass. Pour a table-spoon of caramel topping over the ice cream, and then follow that with a layer of crushed malted milk balls.

Repeat these steps by adding another scoop of ice cream, a layer of caramel topping, and a sprinkling of milk balls. Top off with whipped cream, and garnish with a malted milk ball.

* To make homemade toppings for this recipe, see the toppings chapter in this book.

What's a parfait? Just think of parfaits as layered sundaes in a glass. You will have fun building your parfait, layer by layer, until you reach the top of the glass. And it's even more fun to dig your way, bite by bite, back to the bottom with a spoon. This recipe makes two, because parfaits are just too good to eat by yourself.

## Ingredients:
4 scoops vanilla ice cream
1 cup (240 ml) caramel topping*
1/2 cup (120 ml) crushed malted milk balls
2 whole malted milk balls
Whipped cream

# NUTTY MARBLE MASTERPIECE

## To prepare:
Arrange the ice cream scoops in a dessert bowl. Pour the hot fudge over one scoop, and sprinkle with chopped walnuts. Then pour the chocolate sauce over the second scoop, and sprinkle with chopped almonds. To finish your treat, top the entire sundae with the candy-coated chocolates.

## Tasty tips:
For a personal touch, use your favorite candy or cookie as a topping. Break a candy bar or cookies into pieces, and sprinkle these all over the top of the ice cream.

Try making your own creation by substituting your favorite cookies and candy bars for the candy-coated chocolates in this recipe.

\* To make homemade toppings for this recipe, see the toppings chapter in this book.

### Ingredients:
2 scoops of marble fudge ice cream

1/4 cup (60 ml) chocolate topping\*

1/4 cup (60 ml) hot fudge topping\*

2 tbsp. (30 g) chopped walnuts

2 tbsp. (30 g) chopped almonds

2 tbsp. (30 g) candy-coated chocolates

*Y*our chocolate-loving family members and friends will go absolutely nuts over this sundae.

# Fun Facts

Ice cream has become an integral part of the American character. European immigrants, upon coming to the United States in 1921, were given ice cream as part of their first meal in the new country.

# MINTY BREEZE BROWNIE SUNDAE

## To prepare:
Place the brownie in the bottom of the ice cream bowl. Put a scoop of mint chocolate-chip ice cream on top of the brownie, and then pour hot fudge over the top. Swirl whipped cream on top, and garnish with chopped mints.

* To make homemade toppings for this recipe, see the toppings chapter in this book.

*T*his sundae is a breeze to make. The first bite gives you a gust of mint, while the second bite brings you a blast of chocolate. But there's another surprise! Waiting for you at the bottom is a brownie delight.

### Ingredients:
1 nutty brownie
1 scoop mint chocolate-chip ice cream
1/4 cup (60 ml) hot fudge topping*
Whipped cream
4 chopped chocolate-covered mints

# KING COOKIE SUNDAE

## To prepare:
In a mixing bowl, combine the softened ice cream and the crushed cream-filled chocolate cookie. Form the cookie-ice cream mixture into a ball, and place it in the freezer for one hour.

Remove the frozen ice cream ball, and place it in a dessert bowl. Surround the ice cream ball with the banana slices. Keep in mind that you want to slice the banana into circles, so cut horizontally across the banana.

Pour the chocolate topping over everything, and sprinkle chopped nuts over the top. Press the cream-filled chocolate cookie into the top of the ice cream ball.

* To make homemade toppings for this recipe, see the toppings chapter in this book.

*T*his is a sundae that's truly fit for a king. Cream-filled cookies are the crowning touch that make this sundae a royal treat.

### Ingredients:
1 scoop vanilla ice cream, softened
1 crushed cream-filled chocolate cookie
1 whole cream-filled chocolate cookie
1/4 cup (60 ml) chocolate topping*
1/2 banana, sliced into circles
1 tbsp. (15 g) chopped nuts

# OVER THE RAINBOW PARFAIT

## To prepare:

Spread cherries along the bottom of a parfait glass. Drop a scoop of vanilla ice cream on top, and then add some crushed pineapple. Place the chocolate ice cream on top of it all, and sprinkle on the chopped coconut.

Place the strawberry ice cream on top, and pour in the blueberries. Swirl on as much whipped cream as you dare, and dust with chocolate bits.

## Ingredients:

1 scoop vanilla ice cream
1 scoop chocolate ice cream
1 scoop strawberry ice cream
1 tbsp. (15 g) crushed pineapple
1 tbsp. (15 g) chopped maraschino cherries
1 tbsp. (15 g) chopped coconut
1 tbsp. (15 g) blueberries
Chocolate bits
Whipped cream

*T*his colorful, flavorful parfait is fun and easy to create. Just remember that shortly after rainbows are spotted, they are known to disappear quickly.

# I WANT S'MORE SUNDAE

## To prepare:

Place a graham cracker on each of the four dessert plates. Then spread a tablespoon of chocolate topping across each cracker.

Put a scoop of ice cream onto each cracker. Pour two tablespoons of marshmallow topping over the ice cream, and then pour the remaining chocolate sauce on top.

Break the remaining cracker into small pieces, and sprinkle the crumbs on top of the sundaes.

## Tasty tips:

To really warm things up, try substituting hot fudge for the chocolate topping. Also, heating the marshmallow topping before making the sundae will add some variety to your sundae.

\* To make homemade toppings for this recipe, see the toppings chapter in this book.

## Ingredients:

- 4 scoops chocolate ice cream
- 1-1/2 cups (360 ml) chocolate topping*
- 1/2 cup (120 ml) marshmallow topping*
- 5 graham crackers

*B*oy Scouts and Girl Scouts alike can bring this marshmallow treat from the camp fire into the kitchen. This recipe makes four S'more Sundaes. Beware, because once you're done with these, you'll want four s'more. P.S. You'll love this recipe even if you aren't a scout!

 Fun Facts

The hokey-pokey man was an ice cream vendor. Hokey-pokey is a slang expression that means ice cream and candy attractive to children.

# Terrific Toppings

These days, you can buy a jar of just about any ice cream topping right off the grocery store shelf. You can buy anything from traditional hot fudge to caramel and pineapple. But don't you think making your very own toppings adds a special touch to your dessert?

Making your own toppings is fun and easy. Before you begin, let an adult know what you are planning to do. You will be using the stove to heat the ingredients, and you may need some assistance. Once your topping is cooked, let it cool by storing it in an airtight container and placing it in the refrigerator until you are ready to eat.

# SIMPLY SUPER CINNAMON SAUCE

## To prepare:
In a saucepan, cook the sugar, corn syrup, and water over low-medium heat. Stir as the mixture begins to boil. Break the cinnamon sticks in half, and drop them into the saucepan. Let the sauce simmer over low heat for 10 minutes. After the time is up, let it cool before removing the cinnamon sticks. This makes one cup of spicy cinnamon topping.

## Tasty tips:
Cinnamon tastes great anytime, but it is especially good during the fall months. Try it between Halloween and Thanksgiving to add some spice to the cooler weather. Pour this yummy sauce over a couple scoops of Dutch apple ice cream. You won't believe how good it tastes!

This sensational cinnamon sauce is tangy, and oh so good! On cool nights, you'll definitely come back for more. Only adventurous types should give this topping a try.

### Ingredients:
1/4 cup (60 ml) granulated sugar
1/4 cup (60 ml) dark corn syrup
1/2 cup (120 ml) water
2 cinnamon sticks

# Fun Facts

Nancy Johnson invented the first hand-cranked ice cream machine in 1946.

# CHOO CHOO CHERRY TOPPING

## To prepare:

Mix the water and jam together in a saucepan. Squeeze in the juice from the lemon, and stir. Simmer the mixture over low heat until the jam melts.

In a smaller saucepan, melt the butter, and stir in the flour. When this is blended, stir the butter and flour mixture into the cherry mixture. Simmer over low heat until warm.

## Tasty tips:

Choo Choo Cherry is a sweet and delicious topping. The recipe makes about 1-1/2 cups (360 ml), and the topping tastes just as good hot as it does cold. This topping tastes great when it's served on many flavors of ice cream. But do try it over cherry vanilla, or chocolate, two all-time favorites to have with cherry topping.

## Ingredients:

1 cup (240 ml) cherry jam
1/4 cup (60 ml) water
1 lemon
1 tbsp. (15 g) butter
1 tbsp. (15 g) flour

*H*op aboard the Cherry Express, and try this festive way to finish off a sundae. Once your taste buds catch the excitement of Choo Choo Cherry, you won't want to get off this train!

# OLD-FASHIONED HOT FUDGE

## To prepare:
Simmer water in the bottom of a double boiler. In the top part of the boiler, melt together the chocolate and butter. Add the cocoa, and stir until it dissolves. Add the sugar, and stir until the mixture looks grainy. Cook in the double boiler over simmering water for 20 minutes.

Stir in the milk and cream. Keep stirring the mixture until everything is blended thoroughly. Let the topping simmer for one hour. Stir occasionally to keep the sauce from sticking. The hot fudge is ready when all the sugar is dissolved and the mixture is very smooth.

## Tasty tips:
Hot fudge goes well with a variety of flavors. Start with vanilla, and experiment until you find a favorite. How about mint chocolate chip or fudge marble?

## Ingredients:
2 ounces (56.25 g)
    unsweetened chocolate
1/2 stick (60 g) butter
1/4 cup (60 ml)
    unsweetened cocoa powder
1 cup (240 ml) sugar
1/4 cup (60 ml) milk
1/4 (60 ml) whipping cream

*I*ce cream often needs nothing more than hot fudge to make it a scrumptious treat. This recipe makes about two cups of the fudgiest hot fudge you will ever taste!

# GOOD AND GOOEY BUTTERSCOTCH

## To prepare:

Bring the sugar, syrup, butter, and cream to a boil in a small saucepan. It is best to use moderate heat during this part of the recipe.

As you cook the sauce, stir constantly. The mixture will begin to thicken. When the sauce is thick, remove the pan from the heat. After it cools a little, stir in the vanilla extract.

## Tasty tips:

Butterscotch is best when it is hot and gooey, but you can serve this topping cold, too. This recipe makes about 1-1/2 cups (360 ml), and it is guaranteed to be the gooeyest yet. If you decide to reheat leftover topping, use a double boiler.

Try this topping on vanilla or French vanilla ice cream. Top it off with chopped nuts.

## Ingredients:

- 1 cup (240 ml) light brown sugar
- 2 tbsp. (30 ml) light corn syrup
- 2 tbsp. (30 g) butter
- 1/2 cup (120 ml) cream
- 1/2 tsp. (2.5 ml) vanilla extract

Butterscotch is a fun and fancy flavor that nearly everyone goes crazy over. With just one taste of this great-tasting and definitely gooey sauce, you'll be "stuck" for life!

# Fun Facts

An inventor once tried to package ice cream in an aerosol can. The inventor abandoned the idea because people didn't like the product. Maybe the customers mistakenly sprayed it on their hair.

# TROPICAL PINEAPPLE TOPPING

## To prepare:
If you are using canned pineapple, drain the juice before pouring the crushed pineapple into a saucepan. Stir in the corn syrup, and bring the mixture to a boil. Continue cooking (approximately 10 minutes) over medium heat until the sauce thickens. This recipe makes 1-1/2 cups (360 ml) of tangy sauce.

## Tasty tips:
Try something special. Make the pineapple topping, and pour it over either orange sherbet or orange ice cream. You will feel like you are on a tropical island.

*S*ay "Aloha!" to the tangiest pineapple topping this side of the Hawaiian Islands.

### Ingredients:
1 cup (240 ml) crushed pineapple
1 cup (240 ml) light corn syrup

# CHOCK-FULL OF CHOCOLATE SAUCE

## To prepare:
In the top part of a double boiler, melt the chocolate and butter over very low heat. Once it is melted, slowly stir in the sugar. Continue to stir as you add the salt, and slowly pour in the cream. Simmer for 5 minutes until the sugar dissolves. Then remove the mixture from the burner, and stir in the vanilla.

## Tasty tips:
Chocolate sauce becomes thicker once it cools. This recipe makes 1-1/2 cups (360 ml). Chocolate is especially tasty on top of fruit-flavored ice creams, such as burgundy cherry, or strawberry.

*C*hocoholics unite! This extra-rich topping will get your taste buds dancing!

### Ingredients:
2 ounces (56.25 g) unsweetened chocolate
1/4 cup (60 g) butter
1-1/2 cups (360 ml) sugar
3/4 cup (180 ml) cream
1/2 tsp. (2.5 ml) vanilla extract
A pinch of salt

# GOOD GOSH MARSHMALLOW SAUCE

## To prepare:

Pour the milk into a small saucepan. Stir in the corn syrup and marshmallows. Simmer over medium heat until the marshmallows are melted. Chill the mixture in the refrigerator for two hours before eating.

## Tasty tips:

This recipe makes about 1-1/2 cups (360 ml) of marshmallow topping. Once you chill the marshmallow topping, you can reheat the sauce and pour it over ice cream. This topping goes especially well with any chocolate-flavored ice cream, like rocky road.

### Ingredients:

16 marshmallows

1/3 cup (80 ml) evaporated milk

1/3 cup (80 ml) light corn syrup

*M*arshmallow is actually a plant with big pink flowers that grows in marshes. Marshmallow candy originally was made from the root of this plant. These days, marshmallows are made from other ingredients, but they are still sweet and chewy. And they make a great ice cream topping.

# Fun Facts

In the town of Scotch Plains, New Jersey in the U.S.A., J. Ackerman Coles established a trust fund to distribute a free ice cream cone once a year to every child.

# CRAZY CARAMEL TOPPING

## To prepare:
Using a big saucepan, cook the sugar over medium heat. Stir constantly until the sugar melts and becomes a light brown color. Remove the pan from the heat, and stir in the butter until it melts. Simmer the butter and sugar on low heat.

In a small bowl, mix the milk and whipping cream together. Stir the milk-whipping cream mixture into the sugar-butter mixture one tablespoon at a time until the mixture is smooth.

## Tasty tips:
Swirl it, and whirl it! Make crazy designs on your ice cream with this tasty topping, which makes 1-1/2 cups (360 ml) per batch. Use this topping on Dutch apple ice cream. Garnish with whole caramels for a chewy treat.

## Ingredients:
2 cups (480 ml) sugar
1 cup (225 g) butter
3/4 cup (180 ml)
  whipping cream
1/4 cup (60 ml) milk

So, you say you like caramel? How about eating 1,732 pounds of it? That's how much was poured over the largest sundae ever made. Now that's surely a great treat for any caramel lover! Want to try breaking the record?

## TRUE-BLUE BLUEBERRY TOPPING

### To prepare:
In a small saucepan, combine the water, sugar, cornstarch, and salt. Simmer the mixture until the sugar dissolves. Stir in the blueberries, and simmer over low heat. Stir the sauce continuously until it becomes thick and clear. This recipe makes two cups.

### Tasty tips:
For a European flair, try this over French vanilla ice cream.

### Ingredients:
3 cups (720 ml)
   unsweetened blueberries
1/2 cup (120 ml) water
1/2 cup (120 ml) sugar
1 tbsp. (15 g) cornstarch
A pinch of salt

*F*eeling blue? Try this yummy blueberry sauce, and your spirits will be lifted immediately. Your tummy will be smiling, too. Be sure to keep this recipe handy for whenever you want to let the good times roll!

## Fun Facts

The ice cream cone originally was called the World's Fair Cornucopia. In 1904, at the World's Fair in St. Louis, Missouri, a man selling a waferlike pastry next to an ice cream vendor decided to roll one of his wafers up like a cone and plop a scoop down into the middle. Thus, the ice cream cone was born.

# Fantastic Sodas, Shakes, and Floats

Of all the ice cream specialties, sodas are among the oldest. Sodas are older than the sundae and the banana split. Robert M. Green, an ice cream vendor in Philadelphia, is credited with inventing the ice cream soda in 1874.

Milk shakes and floats are similar to ice cream sodas, yet they still have their differences. A milk shake's ingredients are blended, while a soda is stirred briskly in a glass. When you make a float, you don't stir or blend. You just pour soda directly on top of ice cream, and let it foam naturally.

Always use very cold milk in soda recipes. Chill the syrups and glasses ahead of time, and use slightly soft ice cream. These special touches will make the sodas, shakes, and floats frothier and more delicious.

## To prepare:

Pour the syrup and milk into a large glass. Add the seltzer while you stir the ingredients.

Leave about three inches of room in the glass. Drop the scoop of ice cream into the glass, and add a little more seltzer. Top it all off with whipped cream. Insert two straws and a soda spoon, and you are ready to enjoy an ice cream soda.

## Tasty tips:

The type of syrup you pick will determine the flavor of the ice cream soda. Try different flavors, such as chocolate and strawberry, for variety.

*A* great way to end any kind of day is to make yourself a bubbly raspberry ice cream soda.

## Ingredients:

1 scoop vanilla ice cream

1/4 cup (60 ml) raspberry syrup

5 tbsp. (75 ml) milk

2 cups (480 ml) seltzer water

Whipped cream

# HOW NOW BROWN COW?

## To prepare:
Pour the cola into an ice cream soda glass. Stir in the chocolate until the syrup dissolves. Add the ice cream, and stir quickly until it foams. Sprinkle chocolate bits on top of the soda. Insert two straws and a soda spoon.

## Tasty tips:
You also can make black cows, which are much like brown cows. To make a black cow, use root beer in place of the cola.

## Ingredients:
2 scoops vanilla ice cream
1 cup (240 ml) cola
2 tsp. (30 ml) chocolate syrup
Chocolate bits

*H*ere's how! After just one sip from this easy-to-make soda, you definitely will be mooing for more.

# Fun Facts

In 1952, Lawson D. "Two Quart" Butler escaped from the Oregon State Penitentiary in the U.S.A. Butler, imprisoned for armed robbery, got his nickname because he could eat two quarts of ice cream at a sitting. He was put on the FBI's 10 most-wanted list, and witnesses said they saw Butler eating two quarts of ice cream in a Seattle restaurant. He escaped from Seattle, but he was caught in Los Angeles. Butler told police that he didn't mind returning to jail as long as he could get ice cream there.

33

# ROOTY-TOOT FLOAT

## To prepare:
Pour the root beer in a glass, and add the ice cream. The trick is NOT to stir this recipe. The carbonation in the root beer will make the ice cream foam in the glass. Garnish with a maraschino cherry. Insert two straws. Add a soda spoon. And enjoy!

## Tasty tips:
A float is a float is a float. While root beer is the traditional flavor, give a try to cherry-cola for a zesty and refreshing float.

*T*his old-fashioned taste treat will bring a smile to your lips!

### Ingredients:
1 cup (240 ml) root beer
1 scoop vanilla ice cream
1 maraschino cherry

# SWEET TOOTH SHAKE

## To prepare:
Pour the milk into a blender. Add the ice cream, strawberries, and honey. Blend until all the lumps are gone. Pour into soda glasses. The recipe makes two large milk shakes.

## Tasty tips:
For a pure strawberry flavor, try using vanilla or strawberry ice cream.

*M*ilk shakes should be thick and sweet. The honey in the Sweet Tooth Shake makes the whole thing even yummier and smoother.

### Ingredients:
1/2 pint (225 ml) chocolate ice cream
1 cup (240 ml) milk
1 cup (240 g) fresh strawberries
1/4 cup (60 ml) honey

## To prepare:

Pour the milk, syrup, ice cream, and malted milk powder into a blender. Mix at a low speed for 30 seconds.

Pour the mixture into two tall soda glasses, and swirl on the whipped cream. Garnish with malted milk balls, and then stick in two straws and a soda spoon to serve. Hurry, though, because the milk balls may sink to the bottom!

## Tasty tips:

Malts can be made with any flavor of ice cream. Try matching the syrup used with the ice cream flavor. For example, if you make a vanilla malted, use vanilla ice cream and vanilla syrup. If there is not a syrup to match your flavor of ice cream, just use vanilla syrup. Vanilla works well with any flavor of ice cream.

### Ingredients:

4 scoops chocolate ice cream

4 tbsp. (60 ml) chocolate syrup

2 cups (480 ml) milk

2 tbsp. (30 g) malted milk powder

Whipped cream

2 malted milk balls

*T*hirty years ago, kids gathered at soda shops to listen to the jukebox and sip a malted. Today, a good malted is not so easy to find. Instead, why not make your own, and sip to your favorite music at home? And, yes, this delicious malted goes with any music. Feel free to crank up your favorite tunes!

# Perfect Party and Holiday Planners

Every holiday can be made a little more special with personalized ice cream treats. You can brighten birthdays, Valentine's Day, Easter, Halloween, and even Christmas by treating your friends and family to one of these ice cream surprises!

## CANDY CANE SNOWBALLS

### To prepare:

Place a baking sheet lined with wax paper into the freezer for 30 minutes. Scoop out eight good-sized ice cream balls, and place them on the baking sheet. Return the baking sheet to the freezer until the ice cream is good and hard.

Spread the coconut across a piece of wax paper. Remove the baking sheet, and roll the ice cream balls in the coconut.

Once the ice cream balls are covered with coconut, place them on the baking sheet, and return to the freezer until you are ready to serve them. Just before serving, drizzle just a little chocolate sauce over the top of each one. Stick a candy cane into the center of each snowball's top, and serve.

* To make a homemade topping for this recipe, see the toppings chapter in this book.

### Ingredients:
1 quart (900 ml) peppermint ice cream

1 cup (240 ml) shredded coconut

1 cup (240 ml) chocolate sauce*

8 candy canes

*P*erfect for the Christmas holidays, these tempting treats combine three great flavors—chocolate, peppermint, and coconut.

## To prepare:

Chill a cookie sheet in the refrigerator for 30 minutes before you begin this recipe. This will help to keep the ice cream frozen as you work on the clown faces.

Cut the red gumdrops in half. These will be used to make mouths for the clowns. Scoop out four vanilla and four chocolate ice cream balls. Make these as large as possible for the clown heads. Place the ice cream balls on the cookie sheet. Make eyes out of the chocolate chips. Place a gumdrop below each pair of eyes for a mouth.

Spread the chocolate sprinkles on top of the vanilla ice cream for hair. Do the same with the strawberry sprinkles on the chocolate ice cream. Put the baking sheet with the clown heads into the freezer, and chill for about three hours.

Combine the butter, cocoa powder, milk, and sugar in a medium-sized bowl. Stir this mixture until it is a smooth frosting. Spread the frosting over the ice cream cones. Sprinkle the cake sparkles on the frosting to color the cones. These will be the clown hats. Place the cones in the refrigerator until you are ready to serve them.

Right before you are ready to serve, place one chocolate-chip cookie on each of the eight plates. Set one clown's head on each of the cookies. Place the frosted cones upside down on each of the heads. Dig in!

*C*lowns and birthdays just naturally go together. These clowns are not only funny, but delicious, too.

It is best to look over this recipe carefully. Make sure you have everything ready to work with when you begin putting the clowns together. You don't want the clowns' heads melting during the preparation. This recipe serves eight people.

## Ingredients:

- 1 pint (450 ml) vanilla ice cream
- 1 pint (450 ml) chocolate ice cream
- 16 chocolate chips
- 4 red gumdrops
- 1/3 cup (80 ml) chocolate sprinkles
- 1/3 cup (80 ml) strawberry sprinkles
- 2 tbsp. (30 ml) melted butter
- 1 tbsp. (15 g) unsweetened cocoa powder
- 1-1/2 tbsp. (22.5 ml) milk
- 1 cup (240 ml) powdered sugar
- 8 ice cream cones
- Multi-colored cake sparkles
- 8 chocolate-chip cookies

## To prepare:

Using a melon ball scoop, make 30 to 35 small ice cream balls. Place these on a chilled baking sheet lined with wax paper, and place them into the freezer.

Melt the butter and chocolate in a small saucepan over low heat. Stir in the evaporated milk. Allow this to cool as the ice cream balls harden in the freezer for about two hours.

Remove the ice cream balls, and dip them one at a time into the chocolate sauce. Press a miniature Valentine's Day heart onto each chocolate-covered ice cream ball before placing it back on the sheet. Return the baking sheet to the freezer, and allow the ice cream balls to harden before serving.

## Ingredients:

1 pint (450 ml)
cherry vanilla ice cream

6 ounces (85.5 g)
semisweet chocolate

1/4 cup (60 g)
butter or margarine

3 tbsp. (45 ml)
evaporated milk

30-35 miniature candy
valentine hearts (the ones
with sayings on them), or
jelly beans

*H*ere's an especially sweet treat for a Valentine's Day party, or for anytime you want to surprise someone. These bonbons actually have secret messages on them.

## LEMON LIT JACK-O-LANTERNS

### To prepare:

Cut the top of the oranges off, and gently scrape out the insides with a spoon. Carve out faces in the oranges in the same way that you would a pumpkin. Oranges are not as sturdy as pumpkins, so be very careful.

Softly spoon scoops of the lemon sherbert into the hollowed oranges. Wipe away any sherbet that may ooze out the mouth, nose, and eyes.

Cut each black licorice stick into three pieces. Insert the licorice stick into the lid of the orange, and place back on top of the carved face. Place the jack-o-lanterns in the freezer for a few hours before you serve this Halloween treat.

### Ingredients:

1 quart (900 ml) lemon sherbet

6 large oranges

2 pieces black licorice

At first glance, these Halloween treats may seem scary, but they are really as sweet as can be.

## To prepare:

Set the popcorn aside in a large bowl. Melt the caramels by stirring them in the top part of a double boiler. Remove the caramels when they are smooth.

Add the salt and peanuts to the caramel, and pour on top of the popcorn. Mix the ingredients until all the popcorn is coated with caramel. Remember to butter your fingers.

Pour the mixture onto aluminum foil. Separate the popcorn into eight piles. Shape each pile into a dish. Then place the baskets in the refrigerator for an hour, or until they are hard.

Place one scoop of rocky road ice cream in each basket. Pour 1/4 cup (60 ml) marshmallow sauce over each scoop. Place a chocolate bunny on top of each sundae, and serve to your guests.

* To make a homemade topping for this recipe, see the toppings chapter in this book.

## Ingredients:

1 quart (900 ml)
rocky road ice cream

2 cups (480 ml)
marshmallow sauce*

8 small chocolate
Easter bunnies

2 quarts (1.8 l)
popped popcorn

1 pound (450 g) of caramels

1 cup (115 g) salted peanuts

6 tbsp. (90 ml) milk

1/4 tsp. (1.25 g) salt

*T*hese Easter bunnies come in their own edible Easter baskets made of popcorn. *Here's a helpful hint:* Before shaping the caramel popcorn into the basket shape, butter your fingers so the caramel will not stick to your hands.

# Fun Facts

In 1923, Frank Epperson left a spoon in a glass of lemonade near a window overnight. When he returned in the morning, the lemonade was frozen solid. Epperson had invented, by accident, the Popsicle™.

# Sure Bets: Sherbet and Yogurt

What is the difference between sherbet and ice cream? Ice cream is made with cream, while sherbet is made with milk and fruit juices.

You can taste and even see the difference between the two immediately. Sherbet is usually much brighter in color than ice cream. For this reason, you can have a lot of fun with sherbet's rich flavors and bright looks.

Do you remember Marco Polo and his trip to China? He returned to Italy and told his friends that the Chinese used milk when they made frozen ices. Marco Polo actually must have been describing an early form of sherbet. You see, the origin of the word "sherbet" comes from the Arabic word *Sharbah*, meaning a drink. In the Middle East, serving sherbet is considered a polite way to entertain guests.

Yogurt also originated in the Middle East and is served to guests. It does not contain as much sugar as sherbet or ice cream. Both desserts are delicious and are a great way to delight guests.

# STOPLIGHT SHERBET

## To prepare:

In a banana split boat, line up the sherbet scoops in a row. Put the raspberry (red light) at the top, the lemon (yellow light) next, and the lime (green light) at the bottom.

Spread whipped cream around the outside and in between the sherbet scoops. Sprinkle chocolate bits on top of the whipped cream, and you now have the green light to GO!

*Y*ou don't have to wait for the light to turn green with this stoplight sherbet. If the red light, made of raspberry sherbet, is slowing you down, gobble it up.

### Ingredients:

1 scoop raspberry sherbet
1 scoop lemon sherbet
1 scoop lime sherbet
Whipped cream
Chocolate bits

# A FROZEN YOGURT BOMB

## To prepare:

Melt the butter in a pan. Then combine the granola and melted butter. Press about a fourth of the granola crumbs into the bottom of a medium-sized mixing bowl that is lined with clear plastic wrap. Place this in the freezer for 10 minutes.

Spoon half of the frozen lemon yogurt evenly over the granola crumbs in the bowl. Then spoon half of the raspberry preserves on top of that, spreading it to within 1/2 inch of the edge of the bowl. Sprinkle with another fourth of the granola crumbs. Return the mixture to the freezer for 20 minutes or until firm.

Next, spread raspberry yogurt evenly into the bowl. Spoon the remaining preserves on top to within 1/2 inch of the edge of the bowl. Sprinkle with another fourth of the granola crumbs. Return the bowl to the freezer for 20 minutes.

Top with the remaining frozen yogurt and granola crumbs. Freeze mixture for several hours or until firm. Remove the bowl from the freezer 10 minutes before serving. To unmold mixture from the bowl, turn the bowl over carefully, and let the dessert transfer onto a serving plate. Remove the plastic wrap, and cut the bomb into wedges. This makes 8 servings.

## Ingredients:

1 pint (450 ml) frozen raspberry yogurt or raspberry sherbet

1/2 cup (120 ml) seedless red raspberry preserves

1 quart (900 ml) frozen lemon yogurt or lemon sherbet

2 tbsp. (30 g) butter or margarine, melted

2 cups (480 ml) granola, crushed

*T*ry dishing out this unique frosty creation for an extra-special dessert. And, no, the yogurt bomb won't explode...that is, if you made it right!

**Fun Facts**

In 1946, there were 146,000 soda fountains in the United States. Today, there are very few remaining in the world, except as novelty items and antique pieces.

# SUPERB SHERBET-WICHES

## To prepare:

Spoon the sherbet into the cleaned-out juice can. Cover the open end of the can with foil, and place it into the freezer for at least 2 hours.

Then remove the foil and the other end of the can. Press on one end to force the sherbet out of the can. With a sharp knife, cut the sherbet into eight slices of about 1/2 inch each.

Place one sherbet slice on top of a cookie (on the flat side). Top with another cookie, flat side down. Repeat with the rest of the sherbet and cookies. Freeze until you are ready to serve.

By trying out all of the different colors of sherbet, you can make a rainbow of sherbet-wiches.

### Ingredients:
3/4 cup (180 ml) pineapple, orange, lime, or raspberry (or your choice of flavor) sherbet

6 oz. (170 ml) cleaned-out juice can

16 round cookies, any flavor

# GREAT BALLS O'SHERBET

## To prepare:

Begin your preparation the day before you plan to serve this recipe. Using an ice cream scoop, make sherbet balls, and place them on a cookie sheet. Cover this with plastic wrap, and freeze it.

In a skillet, combine and heat the cherries, cloves, and cinnamon. Simmer for 5 minutes. Then stir in the oranges, peaches, and peach and orange syrups. Cover and refrigerate the mixture.

The next day, just before serving, arrange the sherbet balls in sherbet dishes. Spoon some sauce over each, and serve at once. This recipe makes 12 servings.

*F*ruity and fabulous, this sherbet extravaganza will please your sweet tooth anytime!

## Ingredients:

3 pints (1.5 l) favorite sherbet flavor

1/4 tsp. (1.25 g) cinnamon

1/4 tsp. (1.25 g) ground cloves

8-3/4 oz. (240 g) can of pitted dark cherries

11 oz. (330 g) can of mandarin-orange sections

16 oz. (450 g) can of cling-peach slices

1-1/2 cups (360 ml) seedless green grapes

1 cup (240 ml) of combined fruit syrups drained from the peaches and mandarin oranges

# FRUITY YOGURT YUM-YUMS

## To prepare:

Mix the yogurt and the fruit cocktail together in a bowl. Pour the mixture into small paper cups.

Insert the frozen juice sticks into the cups, and freeze for about three hours. When the pops are frozen, peel away the paper cups, and enjoy.

## Tasty tips:

Yogurt makes for delicious homemade frozen pops. Fresh fruit, such as apples and peaches, can be substituted for the fruit cocktail. You also can try various yogurt flavors like orange, blueberry, and banana.

## Ingredients:

1 pint (450 ml) peach yogurt

1 cup (240 ml) fruit cocktail, drained

6 frozen juice sticks

6 small paper cups

*T*his is a cool recipe that uses two favorites: yogurt and fruit cocktail. The yogurt's thickness keeps the frozen juice stick in place. As you lick toward the stick, you will find chewy fruit cocktail surprises along the way.

47

# Irresistible Ice Cream Pies and Sandwiches

Ice cream pies and sandwiches taste great any time of the day. They are easy to make, delicious, and fabulous as leftovers. So, dig in, and get cooking!

## To prepare:

Spread peanut butter on one side of 32 crackers. Do the same for the other 32 crackers, but use hot fudge topping instead of peanut butter.

Make sure the ice cream is left in the freezer until you are ready to use it. When you do remove the carton from the freezer, take the cardboard carton off of the ice cream. Place the ice cream block on a cutting board. Slice the ice cream into eight separate pieces. Then cut each of the eight slices into four equal pieces. This will give you 64 pieces of ice cream.

Place one piece of ice cream on top of the peanut butter-covered graham crackers. Make a sandwich by placing the hot fudge topping-covered graham crackers on top. Remember, you can freeze these in plastic bags for a great snack after school or as dessert after dinner.

## Tasty tips:

You don't have to make all 64 sandwiches exactly the same way. For example, try using your favorite jelly instead of the hot fudge topping. This will make a peanut butter and jelly ice cream sandwich. You also can substitute your favorite ice cream for the chocolate ice cream in this recipe. Just about every flavor goes well with graham crackers.

\* To make homemade toppings for this recipe, see the toppings chapter in this book.

*Y*ou can have a bunch of fun making a batch of these ice cream sandwiches with lots of peanut butter and graham crackers. Freeze the leftovers in plastic bags for later.

## Ingredients:
1/2 gallon (900 ml) chocolate ice cream (rectangular carton)

1 pound (450 g) graham crackers (64 pieces)

Peanut butter

1 cup (240 ml) hot fudge topping*

# GRAVELLY ROAD PIE

## To prepare:

Pour the rice cereal into a large, buttered bowl, and set aside. Melt the butter in a small saucepan. Stir in the honey, walnuts, marshmallows, and vanilla.

Pour this mixture into the bowl with the rice cereal, and mix thoroughly. Pour this mixture into a 9-inch pie pan, and flatten into an even crust. Set the pie pan in the refrigerator for an hour.

Allow the rocky road ice cream to soften slightly. Remove the pie pan, and spread the rocky road on top of the crust. Place the pie in a freezer for two hours. Remove the pie, and drizzle the chocolate sauce across the top of the ice cream. Garnish with strawberries.

Set the pie in the freezer for at least 12 hours before serving.

\* To make homemade toppings for this recipe, see the toppings chapter in this book.

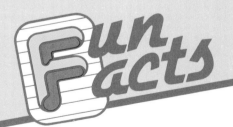

## Ingredients:

1 quart (900 ml)
   rocky road ice cream

4 cups (900 g)
   crunchy rice cereal

1/4 cup (60 g) butter

1/4 cup (60 ml) walnuts

2 tbsp. (30 ml) honey

1 cup (240 ml)
   miniature marshmallows

1/2 tsp. (2.5 ml)
   vanilla extract

1/4 cup (60 ml)
   chocolate sauce\*

1/2 cup (120 ml) fresh
   strawberries, cut in half

*W*hat happens when you add chopped walnuts and crunchy rice cereal to rocky road ice cream? The rocky road becomes covered with sweet, tasty gravel as in this ice cream pie recipe.

## Fun Facts

The first ice cream shop opened in Paris, France, more than 300 years ago. An Italian, Francesco Procopio dei Coltelli, hung a shingle out in 1660, and the same shop is still open today.

# PUMPKIN PIE WITH PIZZAZZ

## To prepare:

Combine the butter, sugar, and 1/8 tsp. (0.6 g) of nutmeg in a saucepan over low heat. Continue heating until the butter is melted. Then blend in the cracker crumbs.

Press the mixture down evenly to cover the bottom of an 8-inch pie pan. Chill in the refrigerator. While you are waiting, combine the pumpkin, brown sugar, salt, cinnamon, ginger, and 1/2 tsp. (2.5 g) nutmeg. Mix the ingredients together well.

Put the ice cream into a bowl, and stir it until smooth. If you prefer a swirl effect, fold the mixture gently into the ice cream, allowing streaks to remain. Then pour the entire mixture onto the graham cracker pie crust. Freeze until the pie is firm. Before serving, garnish the pie with whipped cream.

*E*veryone loves pumpkin pie in the fall when cool breezes roll in and the holiday festivities begin. But how about putting some pizzazz into your pumpkin pie? Add some ice cream for a frostier taste—and a terrific treat that will be perfect any time of year.

## Ingredients:

2 tbsp. (30 g) sugar
1/3 cup (38 g) brown sugar
1/2 tsp. (2.5 g) cinnamon
1/2 tsp. (2.5 g) nutmeg
1/4 tsp. (1.25 g) ginger
1/4 tsp. (1.25 g) salt
1/8 tsp. (0.6 g) nutmeg
1/3 cup (80 g) butter
1 cup (240 g) of pumpkin, mashed (canned or cooked)
1 quart (900 ml) vanilla ice cream, softened
Whipped cream (optional)

## Fun Facts

Always rinse an ice cream scoop off between uses. Also, dry the scoop off because a wet scoop will cause a layer of ice to form on the ice cream, and this is not good for its flavor.

## To prepare:

Mix the chocolate and butter together in a saucepan. Cook over medium heat until these are melted. Then add the cereal and coconut to the mixture, and stir it well.

Butter a 9-inch pie plate by using a small piece of butter and rubbing it over the plate. Press the mixture over the plate so that all areas are covered. Spread the French vanilla ice cream over the crust you have just completed. Then spread the chocolate ice cream over the top of this.

Put the pie into the freezer until it becomes firm. When you are ready to serve, top the pie with whipped cream and even a crumbled chocolate bar if you like.

## Ingredients:

3/4 cup (168.75 g) semisweet chocolate chips

2 cups (450 g) crunchy rice cereal

1/2 cup (87.5 g) shredded coconut

3 tbsp. (45 ml) butter or margarine

1 pint (450 ml) French vanilla ice cream, softened

1 pint (450 ml) double chocolate fudge ice cream, softened

Whipped cream

*F*abulous, flavorful, and easy-as-pie to make, this recipe combines the wonderful taste sensations of chocolate and ice cream with a big CRUNCH in every bite. This is sure to be a favorite.

# NUTTY BUTTER BALLS

## To prepare:
In a medium-sized bowl, combine the graham cracker crumbs, sugar, cinnamon, and peanut butter. Scoop the ice cream into large balls. Then roll the balls in the crumb mixture until it becomes thoroughly coated.

Freeze these creations until you are ready to serve them. Pour chocolate fudge syrup over the top of the balls just before serving.

These incredibly yummy peanut butter balls are great to serve for a party, for your family, or simply for treating yourself! Use chunky-style peanut butter if you're in the mood for crunching.

### Ingredients:
1 cup (240 ml) graham cracker crumbs
2 tbsp. (30 g) sugar
1/4 tsp. (1.25 g) cinnamon
1/4 cup (60 ml) chunky or creamy peanut butter
1 quart (900 ml) vanilla, chocolate-chip, or Dutch apple ice cream
1 can chocolate fudge syrup

# SCRUMPTIOUS STRAWBERRY PIE

## To prepare:
Combine the sugar and strawberries in a saucepan, and heat over medium heat. Stir the mixture until the sugar is dissolved. Spread half of the strawberries over the pie crust.

Next, spread the ice cream over the strawberries. Cover with the remaining berries, and then freeze the pie. Put whipped cream over the top of the pie before serving.

This recipe features both the freshness of strawberries and the sweetness of ice cream. Combine the two—and watch out!

### Ingredients:
1-1/2 cups (360 ml) fresh strawberries, sliced
1 9-inch (22.9 cm) vanilla or graham cracker crumb crust
1/4 cup (60 ml) sugar
1 quart (900 ml) vanilla or strawberry ice cream, softened
Whipped cream

# PRALINES AND CREAM PIE

## To prepare:

Place the chocolate wafers on a sheet of wax paper, and crush them with a rolling pin. Place the crushed wafers into a mixing bowl. Add melted butter, and mix together. Press this mixture into a 9-inch pie pan to form the crust.

Allow the pralines and cream ice cream to soften. Then spread the ice cream across the pie crust. Place the ice cream pie into the freezer for two hours.

After two hours, remove the pie, and swirl small dabs of whipped cream across the top. Drizzle the fudge topping in between the whipped cream swirls. Place the pie back into a freezer for at least 12 hours before serving.

## Ingredients:

1 quart (900 ml) pralines and cream ice cream

1/2 package chocolate wafers

1/2 stick (60 g) butter, melted

1/2 cup (120 ml) hot fudge sauce, cooled*

Whipped cream

You simply can't beat the flavor combinations in this pie. Pralines and cream ice cream is one of the most popular flavors in the world. And when you add a chocolate crust to the recipe, watch out taste buds!

## Fun Facts

Ice cream tastes best when taken directly from the freezer to a chilled plate, and then served to the person who will enjoy the dish.

# Have Some Fun Making Your Own Ice Cream

You can enjoy making your own ice cream at home. It is not as difficult as you might think at first.

There are two types of ice cream makers. There is the hand-cranked type and the motor-driven style. These machines basically are the same, except the hand-cranked style is manual and, therefore, requires a little more work. Both types need salt and ice to produce ice cream. Salt keeps the ice cold during the process. In fact, the salt actually lowers the temperature of the ice, which is good for making ice cream. Look to your particular machine's instructions for the right amounts of salt and ice.

Ice cream is made by slowly pumping air into the ingredients. The ice cream machine does this during the mixing stage. Try to use fresh ingredients for these homemade ice cream recipes. And when you freeze your batch of ice cream, pack it carefully into an airtight container, and wrap plastic around the outside.

# SIMPLY DELICIOUS VANILLA ICE CREAM

## To prepare:

Mix the half and half, sugar, egg, and vanilla in a blender on medium speed. When the mixture is smooth and the sugar has dissolved, slowly add the cream.

Blend on a low speed for about 30 seconds until the mixture is smooth. You are now ready to use your ice cream machine. Follow the manufacturer's instructions for freezing the ice cream.

Vanilla is the most popular of all the ice cream flavors, and it goes perfectly with just about any topping. This recipe makes one quart. So, since there's plenty, invite family or friends to enjoy your homemade treat. Ice cream can add life to any kind of gathering.

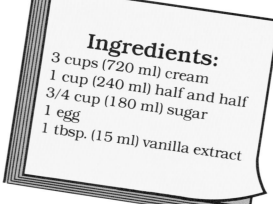

## Ingredients:

3 cups (720 ml) cream
1 cup (240 ml) half and half
3/4 cup (180 ml) sugar
1 egg
1 tbsp. (15 ml) vanilla extract

**Fun Facts**

When you are dishing up ice cream, quickly scoop out the portions you want, and return the carton to the freezer. This will preserve all the flavor for the next time you want a treat.

# CHOCOLATE-LOVER'S ICE CREAM DREAM

## To prepare:

Mix the cornstarch, sugar, and salt together in a medium saucepan. Stir in the milk, and simmer over low heat.

Beat the eggs with a whisk in a small bowl. Stir the beaten eggs into the hot milk mixture. Continue to simmer over low heat for two minutes.

In a double boiler, melt the chocolate. Pour the melted chocolate into the egg and hot milk mixture. Beat the mixture with a whisk until it is smooth. Slowly stir in the evaporated milk, vanilla, and whipping cream.

Before using your ice cream machine, allow the mixture to cool to room temperature. Then follow the manufacturer's instructions for freezing the ice cream.

*A*fter trying this scrumptious home-made ice cream, you may never want to eat chocolate ice cream from a grocery store again. This recipe makes one quart.

## Ingredients:

- 3 ounces (85 g) semisweet chocolate
- 3 cups (720 ml) milk
- 2 eggs
- 1-1/3 cups (320 ml) sugar
- 1 can (240 ml) evaporated milk
- 1 cup (240 ml) whipping cream
- 1 tbsp. (15 g) cornstarch
- 1 tsp. (5 ml) vanilla extract
- 1/4 tsp. (1.25 g) salt

# DOUBLE DUTCH CHOCOLATE ICE CREAM

## To prepare:

Heat the half and half, sugar, and cocoa over low heat in a medium saucepan. Stir in 1/2 cup (120 ml) of cream.

Next, you need to separate the egg whites from the egg yolks. This is done by cracking the eggs in half carefully, and transferring the yolk back and forth between the halves. Do this over a bowl, and let the egg white drip into the bowl. Then whisk just the egg yolks and the rest of the cream together. Pour the egg yolks and cream mixture into the medium saucepan.

Whisk the mixture as it simmers for two minutes. Stir in the vanilla. Before using your ice cream machine, allow the mixture to cool to room temperature. Follow the manufacturer's instructions for freezing the ice cream.

## Ingredients:

2 cups (480 ml)
half and half
1 cup (240 ml) cream
1 cup (240 ml) Dutch cocoa
4 egg yolks
2/3 cup (160 ml) sugar
1 tsp. (5 ml)
vanilla extract

**D**ouble Dutch chocolate ice cream is fantastic! It is like packing twice the chocolate power into a single scoop. This recipe makes one quart.

# EXTRAORDINARY STRAWBERRY ICE CREAM

## To prepare:
Mix the lemon juice and strawberries together in a blender. In a small bowl, beat the egg and sugar together with a whisk until the mixture thickens.

Pour the egg and sugar into the blender. Add the half and half and the cream. Blend the mixture on a low speed for about 30 seconds, or until it is smooth. You are now ready to use your ice cream machine. Follow the manufacturer's instructions for freezing the ice cream.

## Ingredients:
3 cups (720 ml) fresh strawberries

1-1/4 cup (300 ml) cream

1 egg

3/4 cup (180 ml) sugar

1/2 cup (120 ml) half and half

1 tbsp. (15 ml) fresh lemon juice

*N*eapolitan ice cream consists of vanilla, chocolate, and strawberry flavors. You already know how to make the first two. So, here is a recipe for strawberry. The recipe makes one quart.

# TALL CHERRY TREE ICE CREAM

## To prepare:
In a double boiler, simmer the cherries, the water, and 1/2 cup (120 ml) of sugar for 10 minutes. Use a mixer to blend the mixture at a low speed for 30 seconds. Set it aside in a bowl to cool.

In a blender on low speed, mix the egg, half and half, 1/2 cup (120 ml) of sugar, vanilla, and the cherry mixture for 30 seconds.

Add the cream, and blend for 30 more seconds. You are now ready to use your ice cream machine. Follow the manufacturer's instructions for freezing the ice cream.

## Ingredients:
1-1/2 cups (360 ml) fresh cherries, with pits removed

3 cups (720 ml) cream

1 cup (240 ml) half and half

1 cup (240 ml) sugar

1 egg

1/4 cup (60 ml) water

1 tsp. (5 ml) vanilla extract

*K*eep your eye out for fresh cherries in season. When cherries are right off the tree, they can be used to make a fantastic homemade ice cream. This recipe makes one quart.

# My Very Own
# Ice Cream Diary

Here, in your very own diary, you can keep track of what ice cream treats you like best. Include any special notes that you want to remember.

Ice cream recipe I tried: _____

Date I made it: _____

Occasion for this treat: _____

What I liked best about this recipe: _____

_____

Ingredients I'll change next time: _____

_____

---

Ice cream recipe I tried: _____

Date I made it: _____

Occasion for this treat: _____

What I liked best about this recipe: _____

_____

Ingredients I'll change next time: _____

_____

Ice cream recipe I tried: _____

Date I made it: _____

Occasion for this treat: _____

What I liked best about this recipe: _____

_____

_____

Ingredients I'll change next time: _____

_____

---

Ice cream recipe I tried: _____

Date I made it: _____

Occasion for this treat: _____

What I liked best about this recipe: _____

_____

_____

Ingredients I'll change next time: _____

_____

# Recipe Index